D1626835

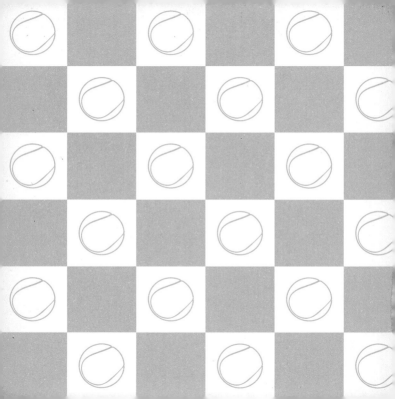

You Know You're a
Tennis Fanatic
When...

MINE!

Mike Haskins
& Clive Whichelow

summersdale

YOU KNOW YOU'RE A TENNIS FANATIC WHEN...

Summersdale Publishers Ltd
46 West Street
Chichester
West Sussex
PO19 1RP
UK

www.summersdale.com

Printed and bound in China

ISBN: 978-1-84953-047-7

Substantial discounts on bulk quantities of Summersdale books are available to corporations, professional associations and other organisations. For details contact Summersdale Publishers by telephone: +44 (0) 1243771107, fax: +44 (0) 1243 786300 or email: nicky@summersdale.com.

You Know You're a

Tennis Fanatic

When...

You consider being diagnosed with tennis elbow as one of the proudest moments of your life.

You use the expression 'You cannot be serious!' in every single argument with your spouse.

You think 'love interest' means nought per cent finance.

You attend a singles' night and take
along your tennis racquet.

You refuse to eat unseeded grapes
because you think they won't be
good enough.

You can't count past 40.

You have fluffy tennis balls dangling
from your car mirror instead of
fluffy dice.

You think 'making a racket' means a bit of tennis DIY.

You have a Sir Cliff Richard
impersonator on standby in case of
rain at your tennis club matches.

You manage to fill two carrier bags
with lost balls whenever you do a bit of
weeding in your garden.

You modify your car speedometer to tell you how fast you are driving in relation to the world's leading players' service speeds.

A pair of shorts feels incomplete
without a spare ball stuffed in
one pocket.

You name your children Rafael,
Serena, Björn, Boris, Billie Jean and
The Brat.

Your favourite food is cream because it comes in singles and doubles.

You pose in front of your bedroom mirror with a guitar and pretend that it's really a tennis racquet.

You inadvertently join a dating agency because you see 'a perfect match' being advertised.

You claim you have only been in love three times in your life. When you were 15, when you were 30 and then when you were 40.

You sit down to have dinner with your family and insist on having an umpire's chair.

You have an entire drawer in your
bedroom just for sweatbands.

Everyone at your local tennis club is bored rigid by your live slow motion action replays of your winning shots.

You insist on a proper umpire even in garden knockabouts with the kids.

Your family all know better than to get
you started on the wood versus carbon
fibre racquet debate.

Your neighbours think that you and your partner must be enjoying a very active sex life, but it's just the sound of you practising your service.

Your favourite holiday destination
is Thailand – purely so that you can
boast about your long Thai break.

You've already prepared your winner's speech for Wimbledon.

You win at table tennis and can't resist
jumping over the net.

You're confused by a newspaper
headline reading 'Man To Land
On Venus'.

You've been a fan for so long you can
remember when tennis balls
were white.

You wear a headband everywhere, including the office.

After an operation you ceremoniously
throw your wristband to puzzled
onlookers.

You refer to the penalty points on your driving licence as 'double faults'.

You concuss yourself after a game of squash trying to jump over the place you expect the net to be.

The craft department at your children's school hold an exhibition of all the things the kids have made from your discarded tennis ball tubes.

Your idea of a camping holiday is
joining a three-day queue
outside Wimbledon.

You have a permanent imprint of a headband across your forehead.

The only words you utter to your neighbours are: 'Could I have my ball back?'

The washing line in your back garden hangs only three feet above the ground, so you can use it as a net while your partner's underwear is hanging out to dry.

You think your kids must be tennis fans
as they're highly strung and make a
hell of a racket.

You are amazed to find that
Wimbledon has a football team as well.

You own a copy of a rare book entitled
Andy Murray's Treasury of Laughter.

You dream of watching tennis every night. Observers can tell because your head keeps turning from side to side on the pillow.

You mistakenly believe Jimi Hendrix was a tennis player after learning that he used to play on grass.

You wait at a pedestrian crossing and can't help bending over, shifting from one foot to the other and blowing on your fingertips.

You ask to have 'the referee brought out' during arguments.

The grass in your garden dies because
you have been putting the covers over
it every time it rains.

You make your kids do a urine test
before playing a game of table tennis.

You think a high court judge is an umpire on a tall chair.

Your answerphone message consists of just one word: 'Out!'

You are able to hear the phrase 'new balls please!' without giggling.

Your first child is born and you ask the midwife: 'Is it a ball boy or a ball girl?'

Every book you own is a biography of a tennis player.

Your diet consists entirely of Pimm's No.1 and strawberries and cream.

You think a Murray Mint refers to
Andy's tennis earnings.

You go to New York, London, Paris and
Melbourne every year but have never
seen any of the sights.

You request that your gravestone be inscribed with the words 'Game, set and match'.

You have a Cyclops line call machine
to check whether your partner is
trespassing onto your side of the bed.

You use a tennis racquet instead of a
sieve to strain your vegetables.

You claim that old tennis players never die, they just become commentators.

Your party piece consists of half an hour's worth of traditional tunes and ditties plucked out on the strings of your tennis racquet.

People suffer abrasions from shaking
hands with you because of the number
of calluses you have on your
racquet hand.

You make your partner take a photograph of you scratching your bare bottom on a tennis court.

You can't even serve a meal
without grunting.

You change your surname to
Krnkovski, so you sound a bit more like
one of those Eastern European
whizz-kids.

You insist on video replays for disputed calls in back garden knockabouts.

You attempt to wake as many of your
neighbours as possible when shutting
your car door late at night in an event
you refer to as the 'Grand Slam'.

Your philosophy is that two wrongs don't make a right – they make a double fault.

You have to be admitted to hospital
after turning the setting on your
automatic tennis ball launcher
to maximum.

You form a tribute act to John McEnroe
and Pat Cash's rock band.

Your neighbour calls out a structural engineer to investigate why the side of his garage nearest your house has become covered in 2.7-inch diameter pockmarks.

You can't understand why people keep
buying you polo shirts just because
you say you're a big fan of Fred Perry.

Your family, friends and associates refer to you behind your back as 'Tennis the Menace'.

You become overexcited at getting an ace during a game of snap with the kids.

Have you enjoyed this book?
If so, why not write a review
on your favourite website?

Thanks very much for buying
this Summersdale book.

www.summersdale.com